The Fight for Freedom

Ending Slavery in America

Melissa Carosella and Stephanie Kuligowski, M.A.T.

Consultant

Marcus McArthur, Ph.D.
Department of History
Saint Louis University

Publishing Credits

Dona Herweck Rice, *Editor-in-Chief*
Lee Aucoin, *Creative Director*
Chris McIntyre, M.A.Ed., *Editorial Director*
Torrey Maloof, *Associate Editor*
Neri Garcia, *Senior Designer*
Stephanie Reid, *Photo Researcher*
Rachelle Cracchiolo, M.S.Ed., *Publisher*

Image Credits

cover The Library of Congress; p.1 The Library of Congress; p.4 *Narrative of the Life and Adventures of Henry Bibb: An American Slave*, Henry Bibb, Lucius C. Matlack, 1849/Google Books; p.5 (top) Public Domain; p.5 (bottom) The Granger Collection, New York; p.6 (top) The Library of Congress; p.6 (bottom, left) The Library of Congress; p.6 (bottom, right) The Library of Congress; p.7 The Granger Collection, New York; p.8 (left) The Library of Congress; p.8 (right) The Library of Congress; p.9 (top) The Library of Congress; p.9 (bottom) The Library of Congress; p.10 (bottom, left) The Library of Congress; p.10 (bottom, right) The Library of Congress; p.11 The Granger Collection, New York; p.12 (top) Public Domain; p.12 (bottom) Shutterstock, Inc.; p.13 Heavy Weights-Arrival of a Party at League Island (engraving), Still's Underground Railroad Records (pub. 1886) William Still/ Google Books; p.14 The Granger Collection, New York; p.15 (left) The Bridgeman Art Library; p.15 (right) The Granger Collection, New York; p.16 (left) The Library of Congress; p.16 (right) The Library of Congress; p.17 The Library of Congress; p.18 (top) The Library of Congress; p.18 (bottom) The Granger Collection, New York; p.19 (left) The Library of Congress; p.19 (right) The Library of Congress; p.20 The Library of Congress; p.21 National Archives; p.22 (top) The Library of Congress; p.22 (middle) The Library of Congress; p.22 (bottom) The Library of Congress; p.23 North Wind Picture Archives; p.24 The Library of Congress; p.25 (top) The Granger Collection, New York; p.25 (bottom) The Library of Congress; p.26 (top) The Library of Congress; p.26 (bottom, left) The Library of Congress; p.26 (bottom, middle) The Library of Congress; p.26 (bottom, right) The Library of Congress; p.28 The Granger Collection, New York; p.29 (top) The Granger Collection, New York; p.29 (bottom) The Library of Congress; p.32 (left) The Library of Congress; p.32 (right) The Granger Collection, New York

Teacher Created Materials

5301 Oceanus Drive
Huntington Beach, CA 92649-1030
http://www.tcmpub.com

ISBN 978-0-7439-1519-0

Table of Contents

Slavery in America

Imagine working from dawn to dusk every day of the week. The work you do is hard labor. You do not get paid for this work. You have a master who owns you and your family. He calls you his **property**. You know that at any time, the master might decide to sell you. Your family could be split apart.

This was what life was like for millions of slaves in the United States. Slavery in America began in 1619 when the first slaves were brought to the Jamestown Colony. Slavery destroyed lives and led to a war that nearly tore the country in half.

Many people worked hard to end slavery. Some tried to change the laws, while others went to war. Some people helped slaves escape to freedom. Others wrote about the **horrors** of slavery to get the attention of the world. It took many brave people and a four-year war before slavery finally came to an end.

A master whips his slave while she picks cotton on a plantation.

Whips were used to punish slaves.

Slaves arriving in Jamestown in 1619

A Fraction of a Person?

In 1787, when America's founding fathers began writing the United States **Constitution**, slavery was a major issue. The Northerners wanted to end slavery. The Southerners refused to join a nation that did not allow slavery. Finally, the men came up with the Three-fifths Compromise. Slaves would be counted as $\frac{3}{5}$, or 60%, of a person when the people of a state were counted.

Slave Journeys

African men, women, and children were kidnapped from their homes and sold to slave traders. They were then put onto crowded ships headed for the colonies in America where they would be sold into slavery. Many slaves did not survive this journey. The United States finally banned the trading of slaves in 1808. However, people in America were still allowed to buy and sell slaves to each other.

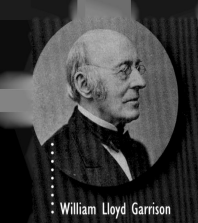

William Lloyd Garrison

One of the First

William Lloyd Garrison was one of the first leaders of the abolitionist movement. In 1831, Garrison started an antislavery newspaper in Massachusetts. It was called *The Liberator*. Garrison wrote that slavery was "an earthquake rumbling under our feet." Just as an earthquake rips apart land, he viewed slavery as an issue that would tear apart the nation.

Martyr or Menace?

Abolitionist John Brown believed slavery was a sin. He wanted to end slavery by any means necessary. Some people thought he went too far when he tried to steal guns to give to slaves. They viewed him as a **menace**. Others thought what he did was a good idea. They viewed him as a **martyr** (MAHR-ter). Brown was later hanged for his actions.

Thoughts of Freedom

North Versus South

The 13 American colonies won their independence from Great Britain in the Revolutionary War. These colonies became states united as one nation. But that did not change the fact that each state was different.

Life in the Southern states was based on farming. The early settlers planted large farms, called **plantations**. They covered hundreds or even thousands of acres. Plantation owners needed a lot of workers to plant, tend, and pick crops on their farms. The owners chose to use slave labor so they would not have to pay so many workers.

Plantation house in the South

Slave cabin in the South

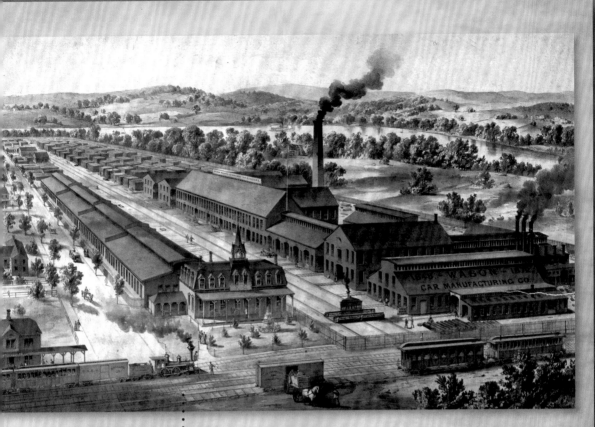

Factories in the North

Life in the Northern states was very different. The Northern economy was built on **manufacturing**. Factories in the North took southern crops, such as cotton, and turned them into goods. Most Northerners made money by manufacturing, transporting, or selling these goods.

Some people in the North thought that a country built on freedom should not take away freedom from some of its people. They thought slavery was wrong. So, they started working hard to end slavery in America. These people were called **abolitionists** (ab-uh-LISH-uh-nists). Abolitionists gave speeches and wrote books to share their ideas.

Women in Action

Sarah and Angelina Grimké (GRIM-key) grew up surrounded by slaves. They lived on a plantation in South Carolina. Their father owned the slaves who worked there. The Grimké sisters were never comfortable with the idea of people owning other people. They believed slavery was wrong.

In 1821, Sarah traveled to Philadelphia, Pennsylvania, with her father. There she met members of the Society of Friends. The Society of Friends was a religious group that spoke out against slavery. Its members were called *Quakers*.

: Sarah Grimké

: Angelina Grimké

ANTI-SLAVERY MEETINGS!

Union with Freemen—No Union with Slaveholders.

Anti-Slavery Meetings will be held in this place, to commence on at in the

To be Addressed by

Agents of the Western ANTI-SLAVERY SOCIETY.

Three millions of your fellow beings are in chains—the Church and Government sustains the horrible system of oppression.

Turn Out!

AND LEARN YOUR DUTY TO YOURSELVES, THE SLAVE AND GOD.

EMANCIPATION or DISSOLUTION, and a FREE NORTHERN REPUBLIC!

HOMESTEAD PRINT, SALEM, OHIO.

Flyer for an abolition meeting from 1837

Outlaws

Sarah and Angelina Grimké's fight against slavery made them unpopular in their hometown. The sisters were warned that if they ever returned to Charleston, South Carolina, they would go to jail.

Equality for All

The Grimké sisters and Lucretia Mott also fought for equality for women. They became leaders in the Women's **Suffrage** Movement. They believed that women should have the right to vote.

Soon after her visit, Sarah moved to Philadelphia to join the Society of Friends. A few years later, Angelina followed. The sisters began writing antislavery letters and **pamphlets**. Sarah and Angelina became famous abolitionists.

Lucretia (loo-KREE-shuh) Coffin had a very different childhood from the Grimké sisters. She grew up in Massachusetts. Her parents were Quakers. They did not own slaves. She learned about **equality** at an early age.

In 1811, Lucretia married fellow Quaker James Mott. The couple moved to Philadelphia. There, they joined the antislavery cause. Lucretia became a popular abolitionist speaker.

Lucretia Mott

A Powerful Voice

After seeing William Lloyd Garrison speak at an antislavery meeting, Douglass was inspired. He decided he needed to speak, as well. So, Douglass began telling others about his life as a slave. He would continue to give speeches throughout his life on the abolition of slavery.

A Special Name

Douglass called his antislavery newspaper *The North Star*. Escaping slaves used the North Star in the sky to find their way to freedom.

A Life's Work

When Frederick Douglass spoke, people listened. He told amazing stories about his life. At an antislavery meeting in 1841, Douglass told an audience of 500 people what slavery was really like.

Douglass said that as a slave, he had felt sad and hopeless. At that time, many people thought that slaves did not have feelings. They had been taught that slaves were property, not people. Douglass proved this was not true. He also proved that slaves were not treated well by their masters. Many Southern slave owners claimed that they took good care of their slaves and that their slaves were happy. But, Douglass's stories revealed the real horrors of slavery.

Frederick Douglass

Douglass speaks while police and an angry mob try to break up an antislavery meeting.

The Massachusetts Anti-Slavery Society hired Douglass as a speaker. He traveled around the United States and England giving speeches against slavery. In 1845, English abolitionists bought Douglass's freedom. He was finally a free man in the eyes of the law. Legally, Douglass could not be sent back to slavery!

In his lifetime, Douglass worked hard to end slavery. He published his own newspaper. He wrote two autobiographies. He even gave advice to President Lincoln! He did everything he could to help all people win equality.

William Still

Brave Pioneer

William Still is called the Father of the Underground Railroad. He was an African American businessman and abolitionist in Philadelphia. He was also a conductor on the Underground Railroad. He risked his life to help almost 60 slaves escape to freedom each month.

Special Station

In 1850, the United States Congress passed the Fugitive Slave Law. This law said that runaway slaves must be returned to their masters. Abolitionists James and Lucretia Mott began using their house as an Underground Railroad station. This meant that they gave slaves a place to hide during their escape to freedom.

Road to Freedom
The Underground Railroad

They crept through the night, scared to make a noise. Their lives depended on silence! Normally, if people ride on a train, they expect noise. This was different.

The Underground Railroad was not really underground, and it was not a railroad at all. It was a group of people secretly helping slaves escape to freedom. The people used railroad-related words so they could speak in code.

Underground meant that the whole thing was a secret. Normally, a **conductor** (kuhn-DUKH-tor) drives a train, but in this case, the conductor was the person leading slaves to freedom in the North. For this railroad, a *station* could be a house, a barn, or anyplace in which an escaping slave could hide. A conductor would lead slaves from one station to the next until they reached a Northern state.

Slaves escape to the North using the Underground Railroad.

The escaped slaves usually traveled at night so they would not be seen. They hid during the day. Conductors were heroic. They risked their lives to help others. The slaves who escaped were heroes, as well.

The Underground Railroad helped many slaves escape to freedom. However, all slaves would soon be free. War was coming!

Escape Artist: Harriet Tubman

Harriet Tubman was born a slave. When she was a young woman, Tubman heard that her master planned to sell many of his slaves. She did not want to be separated from her family. She talked her brothers into running away with her to the North.

Not long into the journey, Tubman's brothers got scared and turned back. But Tubman kept going. She traveled at night and followed the North Star. She walked all the way from Maryland to Philadelphia, Pennsylvania.

In Philadelphia, Tubman enjoyed her freedom. She found a job as a maid. She was now paid money for her work. She saved her money to help other slaves escape. Tubman also joined the abolitionist movement.

Slaves use the Underground Railroad to escape to freedom.

Tricks of the Trade

Tubman had many different ways to trick slave catchers. She took the slave owner's horse and buggy to travel quickly on the first part of the trip. She quieted crying babies with a sleeping medicine. And she got a head start by sneaking away on Saturday nights. Escape notices could not be put in the newspapers until Monday mornings.

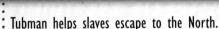
Tubman helps slaves escape to the North.

Harriet Tubman

Black Heritage USA 13c

Wanted!

White Southerners despised Tubman. At one time, they offered a $40,000 reward to anyone who captured her. But Tubman was never caught, and she never lost a passenger along the way.

The next year, Tubman returned to Maryland to lead her sister and her sister's children to freedom. She went back later to help her brothers and two other men escape.

In 1851, Tubman became a conductor on the Underground Railroad. For the next 10 years, Tubman led slaves to freedom. She made 19 trips and rescued nearly 300 people!

Official Supreme Court ruling on the Dred Scott case

Slave States vs. Free States

The Dred Scott ruling overturned the Missouri Compromise of 1820. The Missouri Compromise had admitted Maine to the Union as a free state at the same time Missouri joined the Union as a slave state. This kept the number of slave and free states equal.

Free at Last

After the Supreme Court ruling, the sons of Dred Scott's first master bought Scott and his wife and set them free. Sadly, Dred Scott died of an illness nine months later.

Newspaper coverage of the Dred Scott case

A Question of Freedom

In the 1830s, Dr. John Emerson owned a slave named Dred Scott. Emerson was an army surgeon (SUR-jhn) who moved around the country to serve at different army posts. Scott traveled with him. He lived in many different states with Emerson.

During his travels with Emerson, Scott had learned about a Missouri law. The law stated that anyone held in wrongful slavery could **sue** for his or her freedom. When Mr. Emerson died, Scott decided to sue Mrs. Emerson for his freedom.

Scott claimed that he deserved his freedom because he had lived for many years in places where slavery was illegal. Scott's case was in the courts for 10 years. Finally, in 1857, the United States Supreme Court decided that a slave could not sue his master to gain freedom. Their reason was that African Americans were not United States citizens and had no legal rights.

The Dred Scott ruling shocked Northerners. Their outrage helped get Abraham Lincoln elected as the 16th President of the United States. His election led the Southern states to **secede** (suh-SEED), or break away, from the Union. It is for this reason that the Dred Scott case is said to be one cause of the Civil War.

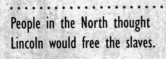

People in the North thought Lincoln would free the slaves.

The Civil War

A Gentleman from Illinois

Abraham Lincoln was a lawyer in Illinois. He was worried that slavery would tear the country apart. He said, "A house divided against itself cannot stand." He meant that the United States could not be a country where some states were allowed to have slaves and other states were not. Lincoln believed the whole country had to be one way or the other.

In 1860, Lincoln was elected president of the United States. The South was not happy. Southerners were worried Lincoln would end slavery. Without slaves, they would not have the free labor they needed to make money from their plantations. So, the Southern states decided to make their own country. They wanted a country where slavery was legal. They called this new country the Confederate States of America. They elected their own president, Jefferson Davis.

Jefferson Davis with his cabinet

LINCOLN'S LAST WARNING.

"Now, if you don't come down, I'll cut the Tree *from under you.*"

Political cartoon showing Lincoln threatening to "cut down" slavery and Davis's presidency

The country was torn in half during the Civil War. The dark states represent the Union and the light states represent the Confederacy.

The Northern states became known as the Union. President Lincoln was the president of the Union. He decided to fight the Confederate states. He wanted to force them to rejoin the country. He did not want the nation to be torn in half.

The Civil War started in April of 1861. The Confederate army fired the first shots. Lincoln knew it was time to fight back.

Four Terrible Years

On the morning of April 12, 1861, the Confederate army fired cannons at Fort Sumter in South Carolina. The Union soldiers inside the fort fired back. The Civil War had begun. The Union would lose this first battle, but it did not give up.

The Union had more soldiers, and its soldiers were better supplied. Most of the factories that made guns, **ammunition**, and other war supplies were located in the North. Early in the war, Union ships blocked Southern ports. This made it hard for supplies to reach the South.

Lincoln wanted to reunite the nation. He also wanted to end slavery. To accomplish these goals, the Union had to win the war. Union troops had to **conquer** (KON-ker) the Confederate capital of Richmond, Virginia.

The Confederate army attacks the Union army at Fort Sumter in 1861.

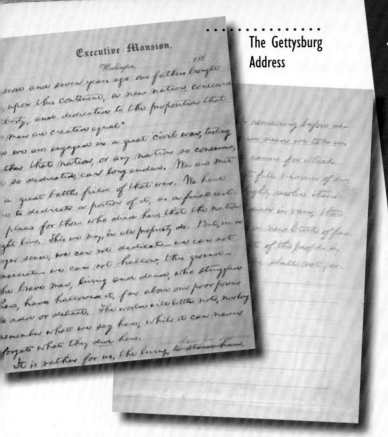

The Gettysburg Address

The Fighting Force

President Lincoln asked for volunteers to join the Union army. By 1862, more than 500,000 troops were ready to fight. The Confederate army only had about 250,000 soldiers.

It Only Took Two Minutes

To honor the many soldiers who died, a cemetery was built on the site of the Battle of Gettysburg. President Lincoln was asked to say a few words. His two-minute speech became one of the most famous speeches in United States history. Today, that speech is called the Gettysburg Address.

For four years, Union generals marched their armies south toward Richmond. Despite their smaller ranks, the Southerners were tough opponents. They were fighting for their way of life. They were fighting to keep slavery alive so that they could keep making money.

In 1863, one of the biggest and bloodiest battles in history occurred. It was called the Battle of Gettysburg. There were many **casualties**. Casualties are people wounded or killed in battle. The Union army had 23,053 casualties. The Confederate army had 28,063 casualties.

Brother vs. Brother

Relatives sometimes disagreed about which side to support in the Civil War. Some cousins, brothers, and other family members fought against each other in the war.

An African American Union soldier

The Bitter End

After four years of fighting, the Civil War ended on April 9, 1865. The Confederates **surrendered** to the Union. After the Union won the war, the South could no longer keep slaves. The Union sent troops to the South. They made sure the Southerners freed the slaves.

A few days after the war ended, Lincoln and his wife, Mary, made plans to go to a play. During the play, a man with a gun snuck into the presidential box. He shot Lincoln. The president died the next day.

Join the Fight

The Emancipation Proclamation made it possible for freed slaves to join the war effort. Nearly 200,000 African Americans joined the Union Army.

Goodbye Tour

A train took Lincoln's body back home to Springfield, Illinois. The train stopped in every city along the 1,700-mile trip. Nearly 7 million people paid their respects to the fallen president.

Abraham Lincoln's funeral train

John Wilkes Booth's gun

Slaves crossing the Union line after the Emancipation Proclamation was issued

The audience recognized the shooter as John Wilkes Booth, a famous actor. Booth was a Southerner and a strong supporter of slavery. He was angry that the South had lost the war.

On the day of Lincoln's death, Vice President Andrew Johnson became president. Johnson promised to follow Lincoln's plans for putting the nation back together. Before his death, Lincoln had asked Congress to pass a law that would end slavery for good. In December of 1865, Congress approved the Thirteenth Amendment to the United States Constitution. This amendment outlawed slavery in America.

Putting the Union Back Together

Fixing the South

Before his death, Lincoln had made a plan on how to put the country back together. He called it **Reconstruction**. Reconstruction means to rebuild. Lincoln wanted to reconstruct the nation quickly. He did not want to punish the South.

But when Johnson became president, he had a different plan. Johnson was a Southerner, and he thought Southern states should decide for themselves how to start over. He had no interest in protecting the rights of freed slaves. Johnson called his plan **Restoration**. This means to restore things to the way they were.

Congress did not like Johnson's plan. It would waste the Union's Civil War victory. Congress made a plan of its own called Congressional Reconstruction. It was much harsher on the South than Lincoln or Johnson's plans had been.

This cartoon shows President Johnson's unsuccessful attempt to fix the South.

BORN TO COMMAND.

OF VETO MEMORY.

HAD I BEEN CONSULTED.

KING ANDREW THE FIRST.

This cartoon shows President Johnson as King Andrew.

King Andrew

Andrew Johnson had his own ideas about government. He did not seem to care what others thought. Because of this, people started calling him King Andrew. After Johnson fired the secretary of state for agreeing with Congress, Congress **impeached** him. He was put on trial, but one vote saved his presidency.

Secret Clubs

Some Southerners formed secret clubs to bully former slaves. Clubs such as the Ku Klux Klan (KKK) spread across the South. They threatened, hurt, and even killed innocent people.

Southerners resisted Congress's plan. States passed laws called **Black Codes**. These codes limited the freedom of African Americans. They could not vote or own guns. They had **curfews**, which meant that they had to be home by a certain time at night. They were only allowed to work as farmers or servants. These codes made African Americans feel like slaves again.

Congress took action by passing the Fourteenth Amendment in 1866. The amendment made African Americans full citizens of the United States. It said states could not make laws to deprive people of life, liberty, or property. It also said laws must protect all people equally.

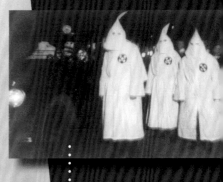

Members of the Ku Klux Klan

A Voice in Government

During Reconstruction, 16 African Americans were elected to the United States House of Representatives. Two were elected to the United States Senate. Three became lieutenant (loo-TEN-uhnt) governors of Southern states.

Famous Firsts

Hiram Rhoades Revels was America's first African American senator. Joseph H. Rainey was the first African American elected to the United States House of Representatives.

THE FIRST COLORED SENATOR AND REPRESENTATIVES.
In the 41st and 42nd Congress of the United States.

First African Americans in the Senate and House of Representa...

The first African American vote

Hiram Rhoades Revels

Joseph H. Rainey

Forcing Change

In 1867, Congress passed the Reconstruction Act. Troops were sent to the South to make sure Southerners followed the new laws that protected African Americans.

Congress made each Southern state elect people to rewrite its state constitution. Elections were held, and for the first time, white and African American men were able to vote in the same elections. With African Americans making up the **majority** of the population in some states, some African Americans were elected to the Constitutional conventions. This was an exciting time for African Americans! But, it was also a violent time.

In New Orleans, a mob of former Confederate soldiers attacked the state's convention. They were angry about the plan to change Louisiana's laws. The mob killed 37 people.

But if the South wanted **representatives** from their states in Congress, it had to change its laws. Southern states had to pass the Thirteenth and Fourteenth Amendments before they could join the Union. By June of 1868, most Southern states had passed the amendments.

At this time, African Americans did not have voting rights in the North. So in 1869, Congress passed the Fifteenth Amendment to the United States Constitution. This guaranteed all men the right to vote. The former Confederate states accepted this law, too. By 1870, they were welcomed back into the Union, and the United States of America was one nation again.

Adjusting to Freedom

Four million slaves had just been freed, and they needed help adjusting to freedom. Slaves had never had to apply for jobs, rent houses, or buy food and clothing. Now they were on their own.

To provide that help, Congress created the **Bureau** (BURE-oh) of Refugees, Freedmen, and Abandoned Lands in 1865. It came to be known as the Freedmen's Bureau. General Oliver Otis Howard was put in charge, and most of the bureau's agents were soldiers.

The job of the Freedmen's Bureau was to help former slaves survive. Agents gave food, clothing, and medicine to anyone who needed it.

An agent from the Freedmen's Bureau keeps peace between angry white Southerners and African Americans.

This is a school for African Americans set up by the Freedmen's Bureau.

The Problem in Texas

Many Texans refused to free their slaves. When 38,000 Confederate soldiers returned from the war, they came home to find few jobs available for them. The idea of freed slaves taking their jobs made them furious. Violence broke out, and it took federal troops six months to bring order to the state.

Higher Education

The Freedmen's Bureau started 25 African American colleges. The most famous of these is Howard University in Washington, DC. It was named after General Oliver Otis Howard, the man in charge of the Freedmen's Bureau.

The Freedmen's Bureau started hospitals and schools for African Americans. Agents helped former slaves find work. They explained labor contracts to workers. They even went to court with African Americans to make sure they received fair trials. Agents had dangerous jobs. Many Southern whites threatened them. They often faced harassment and violence.

African Americans made great strides during this time period; however, they still had a long road ahead of them. They would still have to fight for equality.

General Oliver Otis Howard

Glossary

abolitionists—people who fight to end slavery

ammunition—explosive objects used in wars, like bullets and bombs

Black Codes—laws passed by Southern states to limit the rights of African Americans

bureau—a subdivision of a government department

casualties—people killed or wounded in war

conductor—a person who led slaves to freedom using the Underground Railroad

conquer—to defeat or gain by using force

constitution—a document outlining the basic laws or principles by which a state or country is governed

curfews—orders or laws requiring certain or all people to be off the streets at a given time

despised—greatly disliked

equality—the state of being equal; being the same as

horrors—painful feelings caused by something shocking, terrifying, or revolting

impeached—formally charged a public official with improper behavior in office

majority—a percentage greater than half of a total

manufacturing—making raw materials into finished products

martyr—a person who suffers or dies for a cause

menace—a person who represents a threat

pamphlets—short printed publications with no covers or with paper covers

plantations—large houses on huge pieces of land, usually located in the South

property—something that is owned like land, goods, or money

Reconstruction—the name for President Lincoln's plan to rebuild the South after the Civil War

representatives—people who speak, act, or vote on behalf of others

Restoration—the name for President Andrew Johnson's plan to restore the South to the way it had been before the war

secede—to formally withdraw from a nation or organization

sue—to seek justice from a person through legal action

suffrage—the right to vote

surrendered—admitted defeat

Index

Your Turn!

President Abraham Lincoln issued the Emancipation Proclamation in 1863. Most Southern masters ignored the order to free their slaves. But many slaves heard about the new law and escaped to the North.

Freedom Anthem

Music was an important part of life for slaves. They sang about their struggles and their dreams. Write a song that the freed slaves in this picture might have sung about the day they made it to freedom.